Responsible.
Positive.
Street.
+Rebellion+

To order additional copies of this book, contact:
Xlibris Corporation
1-888-795-4274
www.Xlibris.com
Orders@Xlibris.com
130134

+CONTENTS+

+ACKNOWLEDGEMENTS+

N. Eva Molden would like to thank the HIGHER also known as GOD for all inspiration, motivation, and existence. We would also like to show appreciation to N.E.M., T.W.C., C.K.G., D.W.P., F.D.M., U.D.M., R.G., H.A., G.K.D., and many others for their continued support and encouragement. We would like to also show extreme appreciation to **Blak.Ops.Connections, B.O.S.S. Entertainment Group, and Management** for their production, information, supply, expertise and support. Finally, we would like to give huge appreciation to: the out of the box thinkers, progressive open minded artists (visual, sound, and literary), and those who are courageous enough to challenge the status quo structure and offer solutions to improve.

+GREETINGS!+

HELLO . . . . GOOD TO MEET YOU!

Yes good to meet you please have a seat!

Welcome to the first meeting let's set the scene so you don't miss a beat.

This is the vessel of almost new thought that is broad beyond category.

This is the form of dangerous thought and words lethal to conditioning.

Yep the confession is in!

Conditioning is on life support and tradition is in a coma!

The plug is in the hand and the power is about to go out

All you will hear is a flat line beep sensor and little laughter and shouts

Yes good to meet you say goodbye to racial classifications

Say so long to illusionary time situations determined by pagan indoctrinations

Nope not here to impress or even be agreed with and definitely not here for validation of being labeled a wordsmith

Speaking of wordsmith, is it the gift or the circulation?

Is it strictly for expression or watering down for sheep crowd participation?

So you maybe are getting hot under the collar but it's still good to meet you!

But keep in mind that if you run with the robots and mimics and labyrinth its GREAT to defeat you!

Know THIS!!! . . . . This is not personal and this is not business this is not worldly performance based on limited rehearsals . . . .

This is a greeting to let you know what this is

This is actual revolution beyond what you have been shown and after this you may not still know what it is . . . .

So lets try this.

This is anti-time, anti-idol, anti-race, anti-rival, anti-routine, anti-limitation, anti-approval, anti-popular

Anti-science, anti-media, anti-negativity, anti-inconsistent, anti-pagan, anti-religion, and definitely anti-tradition

This is pro-community, pro-freedom, pro-one, pro-unity, pro-reallove, pro-patience, pro-peace, pro-gentleness, pro-strength, pro-team, pro-flat organization, pro-stealth, pro-poetry, pro-revolution, pro-positive, definitely pro-non tradition, and most of all pro-real GOD!

Good to meet you . . . . we will be here and are going no where until GOD takes us . . . . HELLO!

THE REASON

The reason for expressing thought is not for applause
It's not for ego it's not for the usual reason
The reason IS for the simple exchange of ideas for discussion
For some occasional fluctuation of the traditional function
To expand the mind through a unique system of rhyme
Present some out of the box elements through some verbal and written lines
Hopefully through this . . . brains will be awakened
Infertile ground will be shaken and narrow paths will be taken
This world is relative the rules are only determined by the HIGHER
The rest is under OUR power through choice, interpretation, and personal desire
This is the new dawn of millennium mind freedom
With the chains unlocked puppet masters we don't feed them!!
If you have ever had questions about things being consistent
And why many actions of this world have been negatively persistent?
Through these pieces there may exist a push to an answer
That may help us solve this hypocritical cancer!
As a warning!! This thought philosophy is only for those who are ready for positive rebellion
Those that want a suggested movement and solution to what obligation tells them
Agree or not . . . . improvement is necessary
Where we live is not complete and the results will vary
Each piece is an experience and remains eternal in season
And each one remains a piece of the reason . . . .

THE ALPHABET OF UN-BOXED THINKING

A
Battle!!!!
Challenges . . . .
Devestating!
Education!!
Freely
Grabbing
Hype
In
Justly
Killin'
Logic . . . ?
Many . . . .
Neurotic
Opinions
Position!
Questions
Relating
Structure
To
Unite!!!!!!!!!!
Victory!!!!!!!!
While . . . .
Xeroxing
Youthful!
Zeal!!!!!!!!!!!!!!!!!!!

OK . . . . LOOK

Ok . . . . Look . . . . not a poet
But do like poetry excited by the words
and the expression of thoughts that may be readily perceived to be absurd
See in poetry there is gray grass and red skies and orange rivers
There are expanded horizons third eye reasoning elevated thinking and social, psychological, and spiritual seasoning!
Yep all that is poetry but only if the voice is unlimited
And the vibe is not dented even if the mind and soul is tormented
It's an art but the art is easily choked out!
The deliverer of the message bends the freedom tube and that original fire is easily smoked out
It's like the same color of skin becomes the same image restriction and the message is stuck in a loop
Is everybody hostile against the small enemy and let the bigger one yield fruit?
There are other issues and the subjects could do more
Or is the real problem that typical audiences may not give that finger snapping hand clapping encore?
Then that market should change and that audience should rearrange
Maybe the speech should get more strange to a culture caught in traditional chains . . .
Ok . . . but . . . look these are just ramblings from an unproven lunatic probably with personal issues loaded
More likely more evidence of the obvious conclusion . . . not a poet.

ITS BEEN A WHILE

So the pages seem a little dusty thoughts have been contained
Its been a while since the brain has been allowed to be drained
Plug in the cord into the spiritual data frame
Recollecting the irrelevant numbers and names
Some names are a lil' relevant to fame
Others are ignored and put away with the games
Its the same as riding a bike with the peddles in motion
The same as rocks that's rolling . . . .
The fire still remains whenever its decided to burn on
That light still shines whenever GOD decides to turn IT on
Now that its back let the pen write and let the emotions ignite
The words excite despite invites to focus on perpetual hype!!
This is the actual show and what you are reading is the actual flow
Nothing at all to do with the bums showing off annual dough and rats
scraping the floor!!
We have returned more of the anti establishment testament
More of the fore coming revolutionary ink that leaves marks that is permanent
You probably will say that you missed us when you actually didn't
we say that we definitely hit with seeds that grows from roots that are hidden
Well we are back home so move your couch and your seats
Open the door for some more of the hidden voice from the streets.
It's been a while . . .

+ATTACK!+

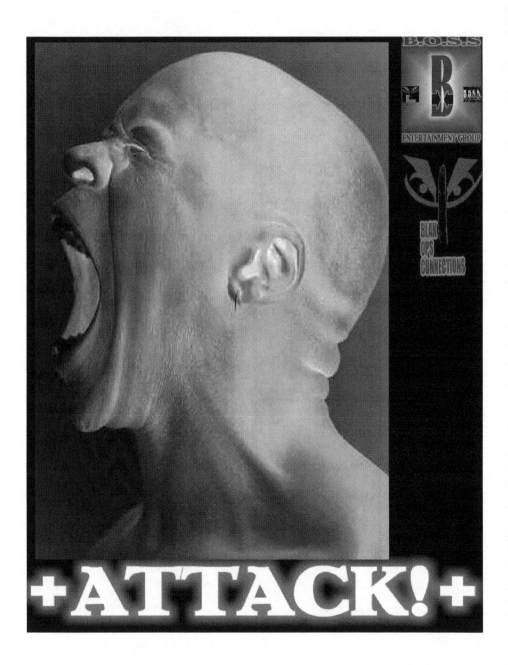

GREY IN THE LAND OF EMO!

Meet Grey . . . .

Grey lives in the land of Emo.

Grey fights each day to be sure that Emo exists and does not change.

Without Emo, then Grey would be forced to move to the land of Black or White and then more than likely Grey would die so the fight is on!!

In order to live, Grey eats the fruit of confusion and drinks the water of selfish and passive benefit.

Take a close look Grey is getting huge now in fact Grey is often mistaken for a stable human being but now that would just be too much to ask

Cows have a lot of fat by the way . . . . and so do Grey!

The difference is that the fat which cows have actually can be useful for others to eat and live off of . . . but Grey fat is just flesh waste and only breaks the body down . . . . and the other bodies that choose to be around Grey

Grey is a host of a deadly viruses and Emo is the land of inadequate free clinics that are understaffed.

So Grey stays sick gets around by riding on scapegoats and fantasy animals speaking double talk and contradictions!

The language of Grey is often spoken by many different individuals who only visit Grey in secret even though Grey is very popular.

Grey is highly successful though!

Grey is the president, mayor, and governor of the land of Emo and has great tourism and great trade with other places.

But as with other trends Grey eventually runs out after being played with, eating poisoned food and fruit, and no longer getting over on other citizens from the land of Black or White.

But Grey is very sneaky, so as a last resort Grey relies on Mother Tradition and Father Selfishness from the double standard pagan decadent root tree and uses those cliches to get by.

But that only works in the land of Emo and the Society of Black and White does not take fraudulent passports!

. . . . Grey keeps coming back though . . . . Emo must have a horrible education system.

That's OK . . . Grey STILL keeps coming back.

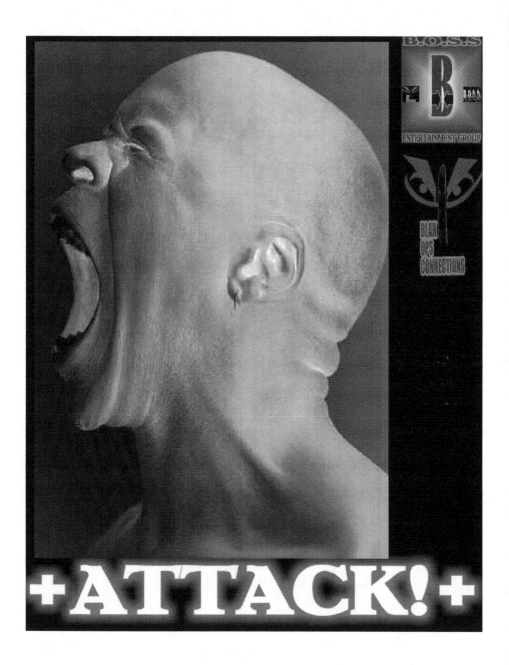

AMERICA

America tries to talk to us and ask us for change
Instead we told her NO and then she put us in chains
After that she started reigning sitting pretty on thrones
Running gossip reports and distracting us with reports of ozone
She crossed her legs and smirked with a baby's head in her hand
She said, "it's not like I care I trade human beings for grands!"
Understand? Its all about power and profit!
Promote social fits with hypocrites in pulpits.
We look at this and are not surprised at the illusion and lies.
We sit back plan our attack between America's thighs!
She probably doesn't feel it because she's been penetrated so much.
We almost forgot she is used to killing without using the slightest touch.
UH-OH! They are sending troops after us!
With loaded social bullets attempting to blast us!
Now she spreads her legs and pollutes the water we drink.
Let's be direct to send this message she will broadcast this all week . . . .
Through media minds that have small brains and quick lips.
Guess they are not quick enough we watch them slip in the noose and hang
on a short trip.
But what is this? We see people trying to save America's life?
We almost forgot again that people want America's strife!
How many pimp smacks do we take? Before we eliminate the fake??
Spotlighting image shapes and cashing checks from juxtaposition to hate?
But let's not point fingers without pointing at yourselves!
America does NOT operate without your ignorant help!!!!!!!
Welcome to the plan for the slave while the chrome is pointed at the weak
Watch propaganda bullets shot from political hustler's speech
That's how it goes from street crime to worker mountain tragedies.
America is its own national catastrophe!

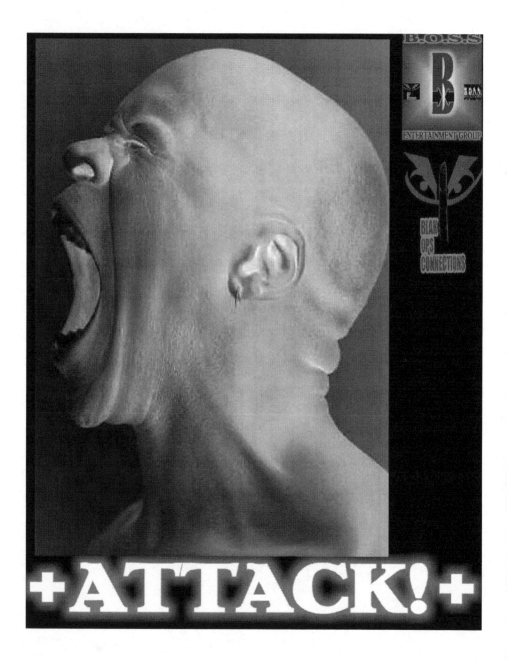

VISUAL OBSESSION

Eyes are inflated and overrated
Forgotten are the other five senses
Shallow is the area . . . the deep pool is a stench to them . . . similar to spoiled milk mixed with breath that is faded
In this sentence . . . . the visual is all that matters and its judged with no repentance.
Yes it's all visual!!! that represents the conclusion
The story ends right there
Whatever else is stated is second place confusion
Basically the world is a visual affair
The jury is ready to attack on the clothes that you wear
Over-analyze you from your shoes to your hair
If these things are not perfection to them they are ready to tear
Release their lions and hope that your esteem is in pieces in their social lair!!
Look at communication and look at media information
Look at the leads on the news
Art is ignored, talent is irrelevant, unless its a visual illustration
Critics with social slaps are ready to abuse
Say goodbye to substance! The roots are spoiled!!
Shells are glorified promoted to encourage image intimidation
Regardless if the inside is worn down due to over-hyped selfish toil
The mass is obsessed with the visual
Stalking and overstepping on the personal rumors
Possessed by physical on the habitual forgetting the essence of a person and the spiritual
Its to be expected its now accepted to be one dimensional
There is huge profit in focusing only on eyesight
Hopefully we will move pass obsession on the visual
And include more senses for deeper insight!

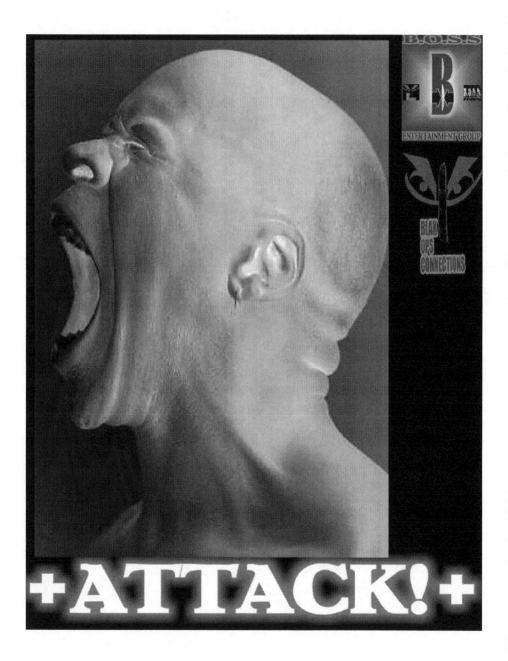

EYES (ICE)

Absolute Zero temperature gazes during the routine.
No smiling No laughing blue gas pumps the machine.
No concerns for another person's situation go handle it yourself!
Sink or swim who cares its all about individual wealth.
Wow do they smell so glad it's not me!!
Now move out of the way you are nothing to see!!
Worthless bum!!! Don't touch this coat cant u see its name-brand?!?!?
What part of don't touch do you not understand?!?!?!
How dare you yell or even think that you deserve something right now?!?!?!
Could you be a little quiet?!?!?! Starting to get upset right now!!!!!!
OK fine take a dollar in fact take two as long as the camera clicks . . . .
Be sure you mention the name and type it nicely under the online pics
Who are you calling coldhearted?!?!?! Is that what you seriously mean?!?!
Who else have you helped today while you support this sick routine?!?!?!
Punching clocks gripping chicken feed complaining that you don't get yours
Driving the blocks gossiping hitting weed insulting stats of whom doesn't get more
Cash, clothes, reputation, materialism and capitalism . . .
Prostitutes, johns, liars, backstabbers,
nihilism and paganism!!!!!
All of this because all the eyes see is ice
Blood frozen heart no longer beating because of that natural selfish device
Freeze! Don't move! They like you to remain in your mental arrested mission.
Just another victim of the eyes visually approving ice that stiffens the corpse in a prone position . . . .

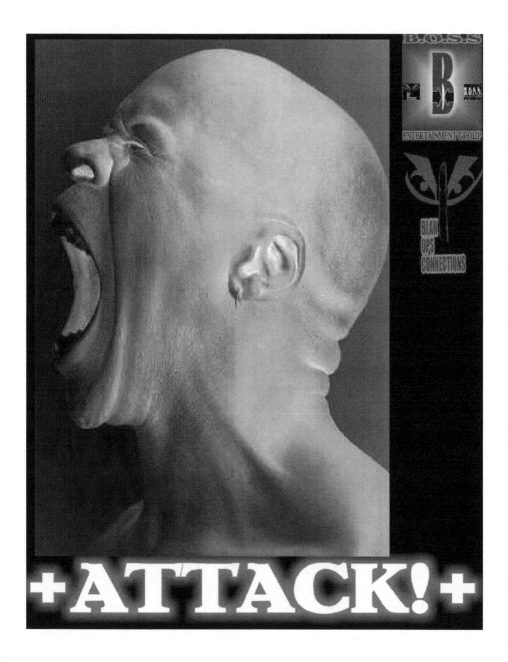

U R A BALL-ERROR (BALLER)!

You get money?

You get paid?

More like your lies are funny!

And you stay played!

If you have so much money how is your neighborhood doing?

Is YOUR wack street hustle business expanding? What is YOUR family pursuing?

C'mon now baller! Remember you run these streets!

Then why are your profit sheets determined by street thieves?

Each selfish image dollar you consume sends other groups overseas . . . .

While you over there stressing over small potato seeds!

If you are a real baller why are your 'custos' so broke?

Why don't you even own your own land? Don't even see YOUR name or a hustle name on that property tax quote.

The real joke is that you only think of money when you want to hype yourself!

Probably to deflect that low esteem image about your over-hyped ghetto wealth!

Realize that you rob the weak ones that are customers that give you funds.

And in return you do nothing for your own community while you give away tons!

Meanwhile other cultures get richer secretly laugh at you in the big picture.

Yes since you backstab they backstab you and that happily rip you.

Your weak self-proclaimed baller status is a BALL-ERROR apparatus

How are you a boss when you barely exist on that atlas?!?!?

Your reward? . . . is that your stressful probably illegal cash flow helps pay serpent community taxes!

Pork composed greedy big noses sloppily moving after getting your financial back split!

Ballers control the game and don't even use a baller name

They are actual bosses who don't seek to claim fame

They have the whole system on lock controlling the plugs on the cash frame!

Ballers are BALL-ERRORS and their mistakes are mental and many.

So please stop giving BALL-ERRORS attention or even one penny!

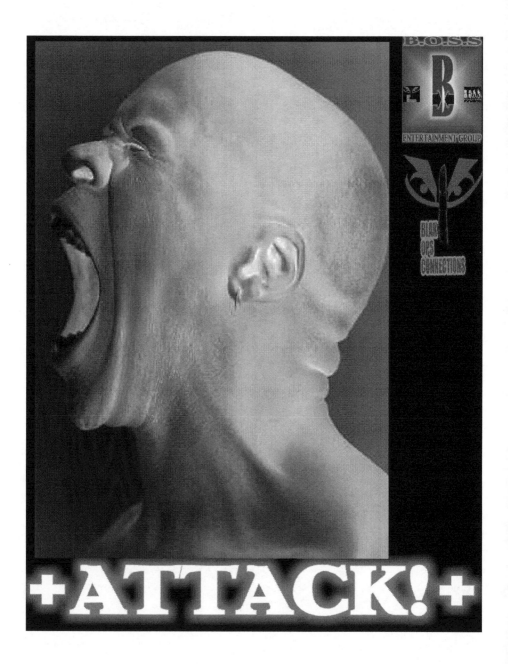

ATTENTION: . . . . WHORE!

Calling all spotlights calling all cameras!
Hurry to the lobby reporters are waiting for you!
Yes its all about you! The press kit is ready!
Be sure you smile for the photo 'opp' and that you hold your smile real steady.
Now did you remember your lines? Is your stage position right?
Are you dressed for the occasion similar to a lady of the night?
Attention: . . . WHORE! we are waiting for you!
We have all the coverage worldwide simulcasting in high definition view!
See how you move with your sick flirtation?
Begging on the media corner seeking strange invitations?
Congratulations! This is your 15 million minutes of fame!
Followed by an infinite amount of light years of shame!
Attention: . . . WHORE! no no no NO!! . . . Don't stop now!
This show is not over!! Don't take your bow!
Your personal virus sucking the blood of involuntary and voluntary victims that are linked to your tactics.
Your vague innuendos moving to selfish tempos ranging from classic to tragic.
Yes Attention: . . . . WHORE! we know your audience is huge!
They like your fake flirtation and your false interludes.
Now that we have covered this event we appreciate you whorish attendance.
We now return you to your regular low class life sentence.

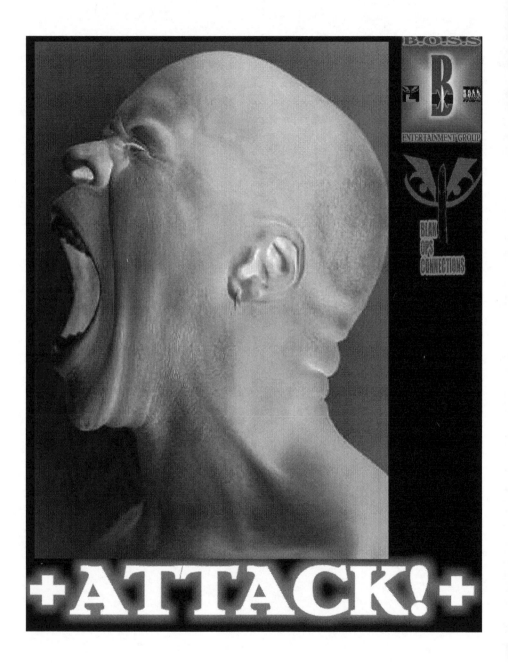

KILL THE SELFISHNESS IN SELF FIRST

hmmm . . . . come save ME amaze ME please ME tease ME its all about ME
its YOUR fault if YOU don't give ME what I want from YOU
I am waiting for YOU to do what I want because I am wanting YOU . . . . but not really
afterward I will blame YOU for MY own problems with ME
but now I am slowly fading and WE is killing ME and US is beating ME down
now I am starting to frown and evolving from a selfish clown!!
but does it matter? because that selfishness just left ME and went to a different host
so its HE and SHE hollerING about save ME amaze ME please ME tease ME
its all about ME
it would be hilarious but is this selfishness really a comeDY?
nope its more like the usual confusion and self loathing tragedy.
the suggestion? kill that SELFishness in SELF first but realize that YOU will be the minority
the majority will BE the save ME amaze ME please ME tease ME and all about MEs

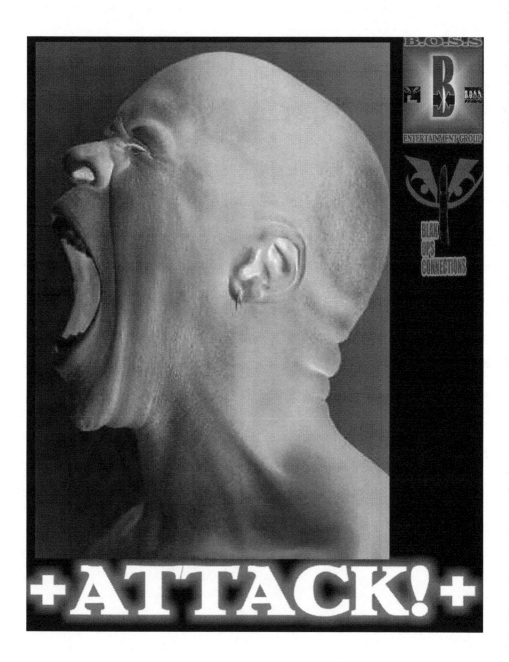

+VENUS AND MARS!+

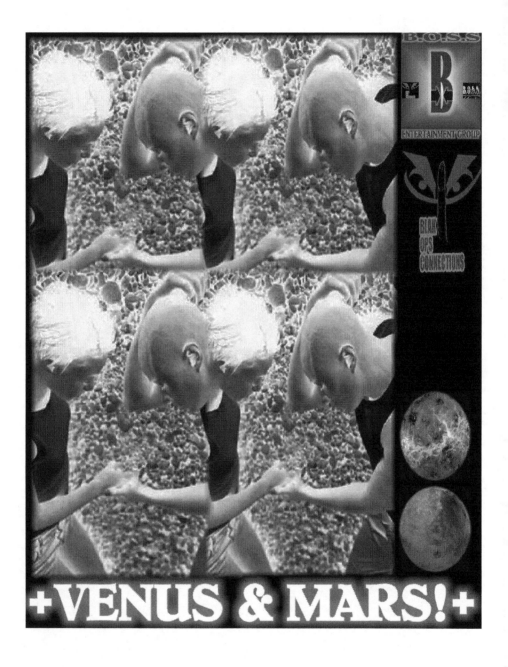

+VENUS & MARS!+

SO THATS THE GAME?

SHE PASSIVELY WAITS TO BE PURSUED
AND THIS IS WHERE THE GAME ENSUES
THE ULTIMATE PLAYING FIELD OF IRREPSONSIBILITY
CLAIMING MENTAL AGILITY WHILE REALITY SHOWS HER PSYCHOLOGICAL FRAILTY
SO ROUND AND ROUND SHE GOES
WHERE SHE STOPS SHE IS CLOSE TO A WHORE . . . .
OH!!! . . . BUT DONT DARE CALL HER THAT
ANYTHING LIKE A TRAMP, A SLUT, OR A RAT
MAYBE ITS BECAUSE THE TRUTH HURTS SO BAD
THAT SHE ENJOYS THE PURSUIT OF A LIFELONG FAD
SHE HAS ATTITUDE THAT SPEAKS THROUGH HER LIMITED VOCAB
THAT BROADCASTS THE FACT THE HE BETTER HAVE ENOUGH MONEY TO FILL A GLAD BAG
ALSO HE BETTER BE PHYSICALLY FIT AND MENTALLY EQUIPPED
AND BETTER BE READY TO TAKE A TRIP TO PLEASE HER SENSITIVE LIPS
THEN THE LIGHT COMES ON HE ASKS WHAT DOES SHE HAVE?
DOES SHE HAVE A CRIB, AN EDUCATION, CAN SHE EVEN COMPREHEND MATH?
OH NOW THAT THE TABLES ARE TURNED AND SHE IS PUT ON DEMAND
SHE STARTS YELLING THAT HE IS NOT A MAN!!
A REAL MAN WOULD UNDERSTAND AND FALL INTO HER PLAN . . .
BE READY TO HOLD HER PURSE, KISS HER FEET, AND GIVE HIS CHECK TO HER HAND
THEN AT THE END WHEN IT DOES NOT WORK OUT..
SHE CAN MAME HIM FOR THE FAILURE AND THROW THAT BLAME ABOUT
SO THATS THE GAME PUT THE PRESSURE ON HIM!!!!
SO SHE CAN BE IRRESPONSIBLE AND KEEP SINGING THAT HOODRAT HYMN THAT . . .
ALL MEN ARE DOGS!

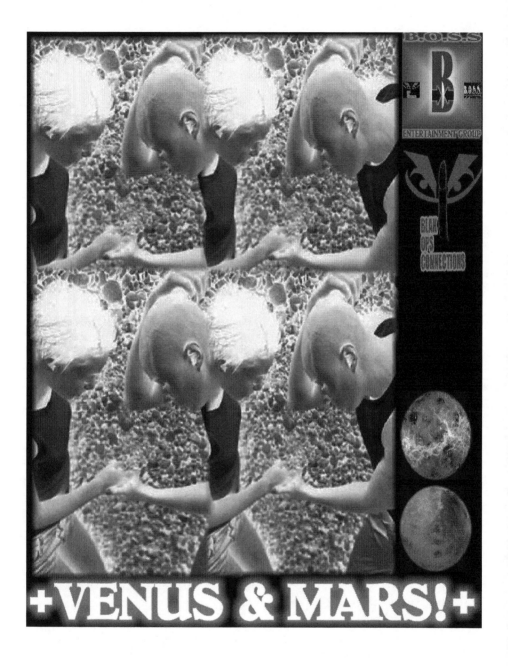

SUCKA STROKIN

He sees her desperate from his lack of results
Also tired of receiving huge amount of insults
He gets lonely so now here comes the lowest maneuver
He decides to heap cheesy compliments just to get attention from her
Hey beautiful lady! You are so fine!
I would do anything just for you to be mine.
He heaps it on thick!!! Deep is that quicksand.
More fake cheesy compliments ooze from his plan.
Let me take you out. I see a future with you.
Roses are red violets are blue with you baby I see a future family in view.
Seems good right?
That emotional fantasy voyage ending in sight?
This guy is just a SUCKA STROKA he delivers emotional strokes that many weak females want to see or hear.
Capitalizing on her fragile emotions combined with her psychological fear.
He hopes simply that her standards disappear
Since his standards have diminished and are left in the rear!
Of course as a final ploy here comes the power line
I have a steady job and enough money to fill a goldmine
Now the SUCKA STROKIN is complete usually she is ready to be his
and when that happens he may SUCKA STROKE the next female with the same desperate lyrics.

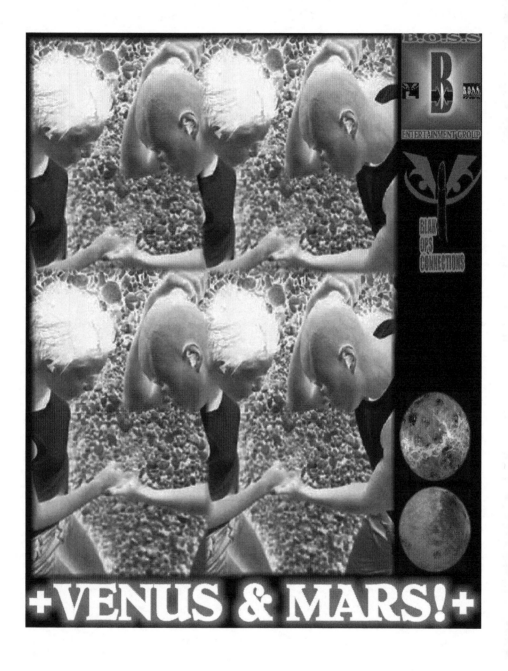

ALL THIS STRESS ON SEX

So let's get this straight
Sex is really this deep?
It's like the main obsession of the streets and the sheets
But WHY? is the question? what's really the big deal?
What's really the big stress on this hormonal wheel?
Talk about sex all day and obsess about sexual ways
Even get real passionate and excited about sexual plays
But usually its just talk and teasing about things that wont happen
Or even went its action its just a cycle that acts like a virus and initiates more selfish reactions!!!
Then its back to talking and frustration begging and pleading for another hormonal connection
That wont end it begins again and the blame spins in a whirlwind
The excuses reign from its human nature to other worldly misinformation
Tune in next sex "time" same sex channel same sex radio television and internet station
Most people their whole conversation consists of sex and being an object
Other people let this lead to the usual promotion of their ego and selfishness projects
So what's the point of this weakness?? If sex is gonna happen let it happen on its own.
That forceful motion usually equals a fraudulent zone
Just think about it . . . real satisfying sex usually happens when its not pushed or stressed so hard . . .
And when there is a real mutual beneficial connection . . . . that travels beyond physical penetration and stimulation
So if you stress on sex then you have automatically lowered your self
Yes!! It's that same self that you are trying so passionately . . . . to feed so desperately!!
But if you put that selfish stressful energy toward what your character contains
What your conversation maintains and the foundation that remains
Then as you develop satisfying sex happens automatically because you have become stronger!
Because your essence is longer and your internal strength speaks louder!!
That's the real climax and nothing is better!
Because it pleases more than just genitals and personal residuals!!!!
Now BOTH partners are pleased from a mutual connection.
And now sex is not stressed because there is now real care and mutual affection.

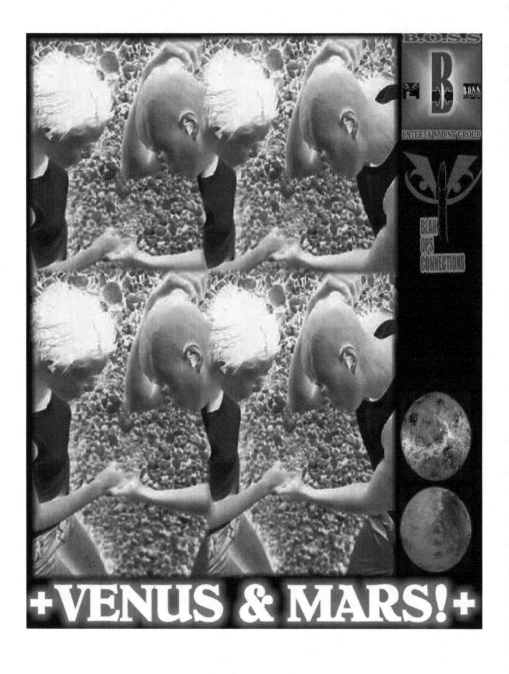

THIS ONE IS CALLED WHY NOT? . . . .

its night and the streets are whispering
the fright and lights are slowly disappearing
five eyes strike suspicion while the mission continues
backseats struggle to contain the members on the menu
we duck down intoxicated by the sweet low key sounds
tantalized by how we are found and consistently we pound
this must be taboo and after further analysis its found to be true
this rendezvous simulates voodoo with nothing but passion in view
so that's it we are in afterglow as the shine settles
for this competition we both are winners and we give each other medals
the understanding is deep beyond the hypocritical sight
so why not enjoy ourselves in this enjoyable night.

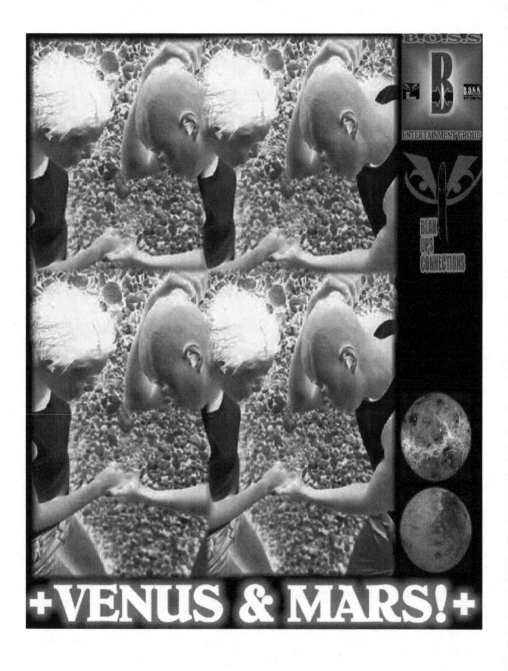

+VENUS & MARS!+

SELFISH . . . . ARE THEY EVEN SURE?

Which do they want?

Are they even sure?

They request above their own standards to hide the fact that they are insecure.

They speak of being fair but not being fair at the beginning.

They speak of telling the truth but would rather lie when it's ending.

So which do they want?

Are they even sure?

They place pressure on reception while giving nothing its clear their agenda is impure.

They are not satisfied with down the middle they want to get over.

They claim to be open-minded but they would rather benefit from gender exposure.

Simply because of gender identity that is supposed to lead to automatic entitlement?

Females are the objects of possession and males are the hunters in the session?

Wow!!! This would be hilarious if the joke wasn't so dark.

And if both participants wouldn't get consistently socially, psychologically, mentally, and spiritually ripped apart!!

To be clear this is bigger than a complaint for this is a solution.

A simple resolution that will yield a GROWN conclusion.

Both should put in to the situation from the beginning so that Both will get out.

Both should look out for the other and Both should go the fair route.

Both should work on self and lift the standards higher.

Both should squelch the fire of selfish desire.

Both should move on from some of the selfish ways they were raised.

And be sure that Both benefit and not only one is getting praised.

To be sure Both should ask the question whats in it for the other?

And actually build to caring for one another!

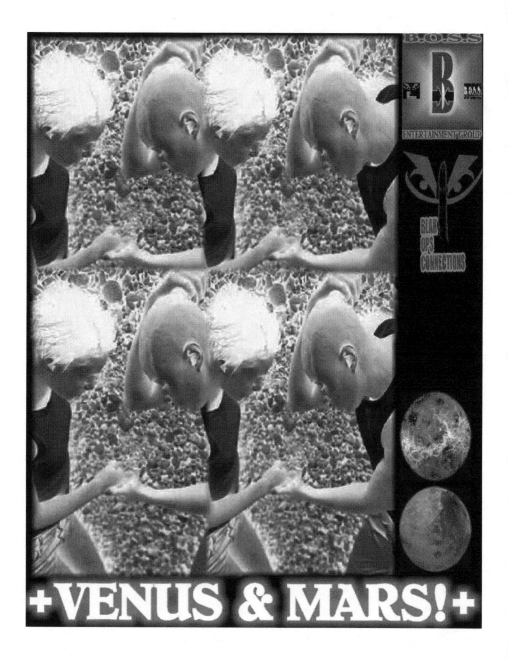

CONVERSATION CONNECTION

Your conversation was an immediate arousal in the evening
Your vibe was even more spice added to our social meeting
Your looks was the same as monuments and portraits by notable greats
Now we are ready to connect and for this risk to take
Yes! Ease into these arms that have been yearning for you
Yearning for more than your physical view and those erotic actions that you want to do
See to be honest we have already have completed the cycle of our confirmation
We engaged in verbal and sonic penetration that resulted in psychological exaltation.
Yes! That smile those low cut eyes recollecting what and where we both connect.
Those miles that we have travel to get to this point of cause and effect.
Shhhh . . . You want to speak . . . relax and just let your mind ease
This is the other form of pleasure for both of us to rightfully complete!
Now your body is glistening against mine as we both physically combine
And because we went conversationally first what we write without words is better line by line
Your flexibility ready to receive whats offered in understanding
The strength controlling your being as both of our pleasure is outstanding
The eyes roll back both of our bodies our heaving
Then both of our eyes connect in eruptions that we both are barely believing
Now for the afterglow the embrace after the completion of expression
Imagine what will happen next after our conversation connection!

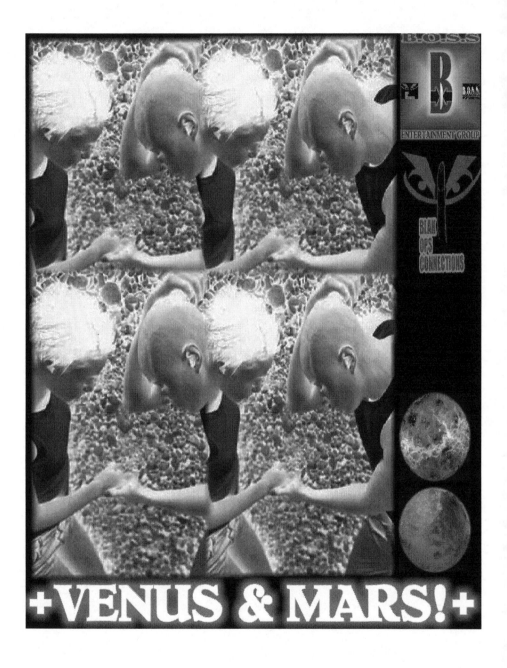

KINGS!

Fathers, Brothers, and Citizens lend your eyes!
Crowns are ready to place on the heads of KINGS! on the rise!
They are the leaders and yes they are still out there.
You can find them humble to the HIGHER and leading positive warfare.
They battle not against flesh and blood
They rattle spots for the sake of maintaining a progressive neighborhood.
Initiating the family helping and stabilizing the structure
The HIGHER is the real leader flowing through KINGS! QUEENS! can feel it
when he touches her
KINGS! are KINGS! and its completely obvious without speaking
While females search for males, KINGS! are seeking the HIGHER being.
What is work for males, KINGS! do naturally.
Protect, choose to provide . . . be a vessel of strength automatically.
Their minds, hearts, souls, and choices are royally fixed.
Failure, contradictions, deceptions, and wickedness with them don't mix!
KINGS! are ready to be a major part of what feeds the land
Helpful with the tactics to keep orders and plans.
Spiritual fruit including love, joy, and peace
Patience, kindness, gentleness, control and selfless prayers that don't cease.
Are the jewels of the crown KINGS! wear with that consistent shine.
Even better is that the HIGHER lives in the KINGS! soul, heart, and mind!

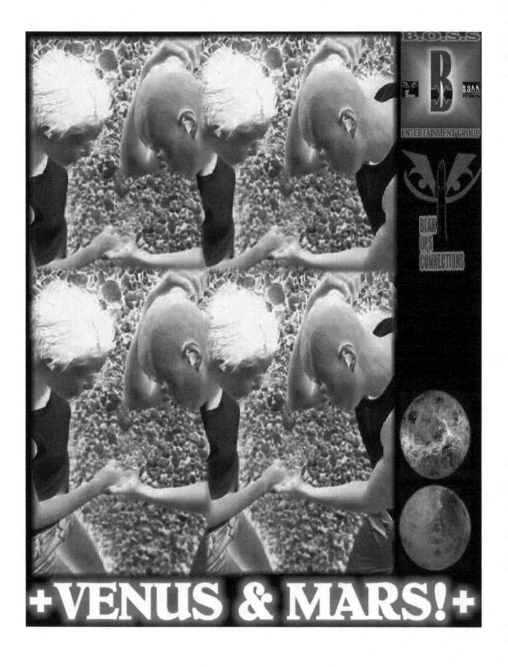

QUEENS!

Walk the red carpet.
You deserve it!
Beyond sapphires and diamonds!
How beautiful your mind is!!
Your conversation curvaceous your character vibe exquisite!
What a privilege and a testimony from the higher just to see you glisten in the internal vision!
There are girls, females, women, and Queens!
Queens! are the ultimate diverse sophistication evident even without vocal commercialization.
Queens! don't broadcast, don't brag, don't self-promote.
Queens! are recognized without even a personal word or quote.
The walk is the evidence her talk is nothing but relevant.
She is blessed with that HIGHER approval with consistent developing testaments.
She shares she gives she accepts . . . . . .
and KINGS! that exist with her mutually protects
She is a partner not an expense . . . . . .
She seeks the real KINGDOM over even seeing a worldly sentence!
How beautiful is she . . . spiritually beyond her imperfections!
How wonderful is the HIGHER that is eternal in her sections!
Physical definition is eliminated! Queens! are wayyyyyy beyond the body and face.
Queens! are fair, mutual, and contribute to any royal place.
The most incredible quality that is seen as she sits on her throne . . . .
Queens! initiate, motivate, and have a mind of their own!

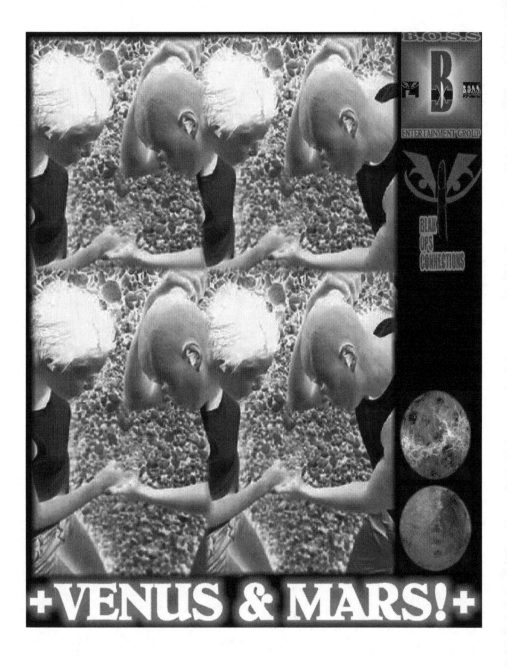

+RESPONSIBILITY!!+

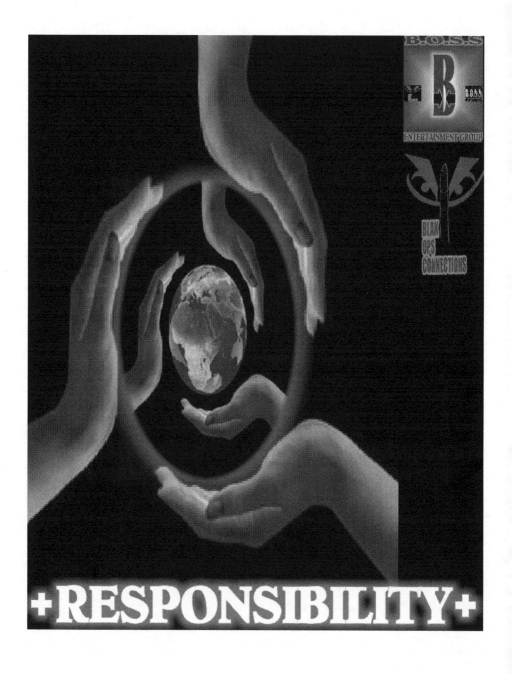

ITS YOU!!!! . . . YES ITS YOU!!!

ITS YOU!!!
YOU complain about gold diggers but YOU consistently end up with gold diggers. ITS YOU!!
YOU are sick of being abused but YOU are consistently abused. ITS YOU!!
YOU are sick of being lied to but YOU smile when you are lied to. ITS YOU!!
YOU are sick of being unemployed but YOU consistently do nothing to be employed. ITS YOU!!
YOU are tired of being lonely but YOU consistently see yourself as being lonely. ITS YOU!!
YOU are tired of dealing with rats OR bums but YOU consistently accept rats AND bums. ITS YOU!!
YOU want someone with high esteem but YOU consistently have low esteem. ITS YOU!!
YOU want someone who is physically and mentally attractive but YOU consistently have ugliness inside that travels outside. ITS YOU!!
YOU want someone who is erotic and performs very well but YOU consistently stay disconnected with selfish clientele. ITS YOU!!
YOU are tired of failing but YOU consistently do nothing to succeed only keep complaining. ITS YOU!!
YOU are tired of being bored but YOU are consistently bored. ITS YOU!!
YOU are tired of sluts but YOU consistently stay in social and sexual situations with sluts. ITS YOU!!
YOU are tired of the same ole song but YOU consistently listen, support, and buy the same ole song. ITS YOU!!
YOU are trying to find GOD but YOU consistently look away from GOD. ITS YOU!!
YOU are tired of people but YOU consistently look for approval from people. ITS YOU!!
YOU are tired of gossip about YOU but YOU consistently are excited about gossip that doesn't involve YOU . . . ITS YOU DEFINTELY ITS YOU!!
YOU want more but YOU consistently don't handle your less.
YOU say you want peace but YOU consistently are sensitive to stress.
YOU say don't like the government but YOU consistently bow down to their inconsistent law.
YOU say you strive for perfection but YOU consistently choose not to work on your flaws.
SO at the end of the day put your excuses away.
There is no one else to blame.
ITS YOU!!

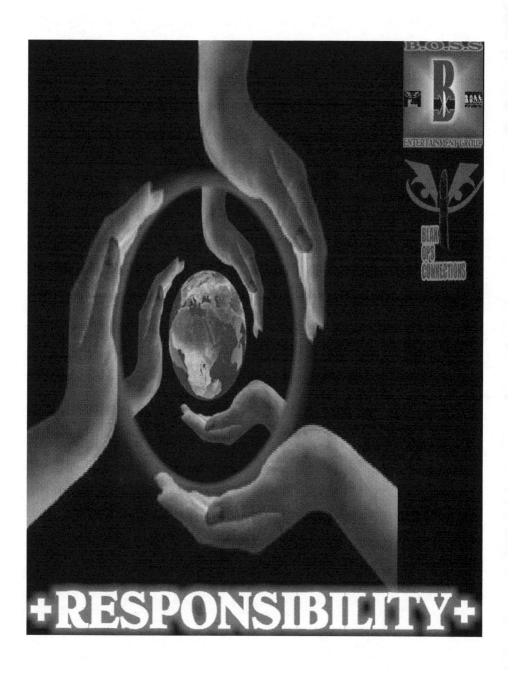

MAYBE IF YOU DIDNT SO-CALLED HATE YOU WOULDN'T GET SO-CALLED HATED ON

The streets are singing the same ole song
Promoting their own wrong and the complaint list is long
But look very closely they are the source of their own wrong . . .
MAYBE IF YOU DIDNT SO-CALLED HATE YOU WOULDNT GET SO-CALLED HATED ON
You can find him in conversation delivering trash
Full of negativity embracing the crab barrel task
But now their is someone else talking him down and wearing a mask
MAYBE IF YOU DIDNT SO-CALLED HATE YOU WOULDNT GET SO-CALLED HATED ON
She finds competition and other chicks don't even know they are participating
Here we go again with this so-called hating
But she is paranoid with a little private conversation
MAYBE IF YOU DIDNT SO-CALLED HATE YOU WOULDNT GET SO-CALLED HATED ON
The actual word hate means that you are willing in one form to die
Just to see that what is existing no longer has a place to multiply
So actually do you really hate or just programmed with a lie?
MAYBE IF YOU DIDNT SO-CALLED HATE YOU WOULDNT GET SO-CALLED HATED ON
Hypocrisy lives in the mind of the so-called victim
If you deliver venom don't complain when you are hit with the venom
The solution is to get that venom out of your own system
MAYBE IF YOU DIDNT SO-CALLED HATE YOU WOULDNT GET SO-CALLED HATED ON
So with all of the issues that stay consistently unresolved
With the low-self esteem foundation mentality that this world revolves
You have an opportunity to be the answer to your own problem being solved because . . .
IF YOU DONT SO-CALL HATE THEN YOU WONT SO-CALLED GET HATED ON!

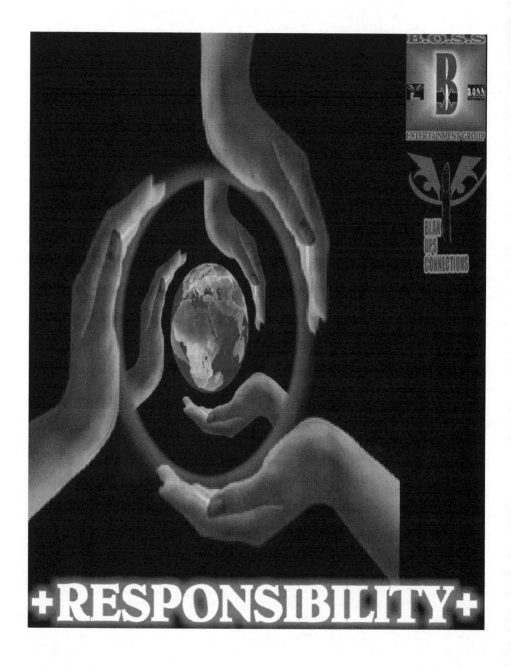

+CHALLENGE+

POSITIVE READ

Yeah . . . . you have been told that it is something weak
Something that shows that your position is too meek
But you were shown wrong . . . .
That lie has been said and written too long!!
You have been told that it shows you are afraid
That only if you aggressively react do you show to be brave
But brave is not that! No it's the opposite
Freedom defeats the slave's mind and destroys the aggressive composite . . . .
Of course you will be sold that its better to fight
With bare knuckles or with physical bullets that travel in flight
But the truth is instead the real battle is in the head
That determines where you are and on what path you tread
So its not turning the other cheek its turning on another mode
It moving through the obstacles and letting nothing stop your joy to unload
It takes more strength to positively care than it does to be unfeeling . . .
Take more courage to let the negative pass than to let off a violent blast!!
Now the definition has been illustrated and the choice is in your mind
You can be negative and choose to bleed or be truly positive to dominate
this so-called time.

What's Your Reason?

Words go by you watch the screen
Comfortably set in your online dream
You are missing many things it seems
The same things that you are probably searching for in the social scene
Now there are chat rooms full of different personalities
Social accidents and emotional fatalities
In these same chat rooms there is beautiful conversation from strangers
Some with intelligence some with temperance.
All of these things are decent and ok in order, but
a problem arises when the romantic and emotional take over
The posts become billboards and secret messages become seduction
All for the sake of desperate people selfishly wanting something
Why? Strictly for the perceived appearance of being in the demand.
With a brain and a plan in addition to possibly having money in the hand.
So here they come! Posting and saying whatever it takes on the screen and the phone.
Just for the sake of belonging and following a trend in the cyber zone.
The deception is elevated the illusion on steroids just for the sake to gather private information.
Offers of sexual invitations just to link with a supposed celebrity status situation.
There is no thought of mutual benefit or even the desire to discover the person.
Just lonely people doing, posting and saying whatever to engage in an online endeavor.
The chess game becomes the stumbled steps of the lame
The board is contaminated because of the hypocrisy contained.
The solution is simple you will be examined and your response measured carefully.
You will be removed and eliminated while direct and mutual people move in swiftly.
There are too many options, people, and methods that exist.
So it will be easy to cast-off many of the fraudulent off of the close knit list.
After reading this, what's your reason for engaging in flirtation?
What's your reason for seeking attention and off line communication?
You are welcome to respond and the verbal will be considered
However, if your actions don't match up then swift separating action will be delivered.
So . . . What's your real reason?

MILLENIUM MACKIN

Listen! . . . Somebody can show up in a burlap sack
With no name brands and a plain shirt to the back
Will still show up and get it automatically
Will still flow out of ruts and not sweat it and live tragically
Yeah this is easy because the marks want to be served
It takes a strong choice to not serve because there is more that is deserved.
It takes no effort just the decision to be
Originally, organically, and authentically unique
That's right! No flash No dash No mush No mash
No bull No shell No slush No trash
All that happens is showing up and speaking
And the next thing known is the recognition of being surrounded by many who are seeking
No slick lines intertwined with victimous minds
Just direct sounds of mental chimes that travel beyond times
The opposite sex is visually paralyzed and there hasn't even been any effort
Imagine if just one percent more was used to put water to desire's desert?
See thats real mackin when the mackin is not intentional
The results are residual, internal, spiritual, physical, and mental.
Many speak of pimping and then have to broadcast
That shows that in reality their advertisements wont last
Other speak of mackin after seeing a mass media fad
Its probably because inside their conflict is really going mad
But this is millenium mackin a win-win situation
Its the combination of conversation, delivery, respect, patience, and mutual anticipation.

FEELINGS

We step lightly we even lie
Just to protect fragile feelings in life
We avoid our own speech because of confused teachings of respect
We avoid our own thoughts because of fear of being a reject!!
These feelings have a pulse that consumes the whole body
That becomes oversensitive hormones that weaken our society
Now this eggshell walking and this deceptive talking
These fake conclusions based on stories from frauds and thin screen plotting
Has lead to lies being the norm and actuality being offensive
Anything less than acting leads to the mainstream being defensive
Three dollar bills two sided faces and one double edge sword
Four angled locked in boxes triple crossed with double agents and one reason with one word
That reason is . . . . feelings . . . that's why we accept the low level
Why we refuse to communicate rock statements and we settle for pebbles!
Let's not forget . . . it's not the actual feelings we protect
Because we already feel whatever we feel whether or not we deliver that emotional object!
So what will YOU do? Will you chose fragile feelings or something closer to truth?
Will you choose selfishness to protect a fake foundation or actually choose unselfishness to learn from individual proof?
Before we inflate this concern over feelings lets internally strengthen ourselves!!
To not be so concerned with the opinions and prospective of what others tell
Yes as humans we have feelings and that is no issue
But also as humans it's up to that individual to emotionally manage their OWN feelings with others attempt to verbally hit you.
At the end, as we engage with social dealings
Let's work more toward personal emotional stability instead of protecting others' fragile FEELINGS.

HAVE YOU EVER THOUGHT?

So we really have to wait?
We really have to wait for calendar dates?
Who decides when we are supposed to start over?
Why do we wait to appreciate who we call a great leader?
Why do we wait to express passion and only when someone or something tells us to?
We really have to wait to enjoy green on the scene?
Or enjoy a hopefully harmless joke to avoid being mean?
Even down to saluting a country's own flag?
Or waiting to reflect on supposed independence we have?
Of course it can be agreed that each action has its season.
But it should also be noted that if that action is really apart of us it should be
constant appreciation that exists beyond just an occasional reason!
Don't we labor every single day?
Work hard and a few work smart in many different ways?
Why not dress in different costumes when YOU decide to?
Do you really require a reminder of what or whom to give thanks to?
Most importantly, If you believe in what you believe in there is no rest from that.
It should be completely unnecessary to wait for a schedule for a belief format.
So have you actual thought? Or do you just follow?
Where is your leadership? Or is your individuality hollow?
Establish your own answer . . . and THINK FOR YOURSELF!
Have you ever thought about doing that?

REALLY? . . . HISTORY?

Track Record?
History?
What really is proven by that?
What really can we conclude from that usual format?
The most that can be established is whatever we choose to conclude
But just because we conclude does not mean it's the truth.
Confusing popularity with reality?
What if each person in that big group was mistaken? Now what happens to reality?
Each piece of information is biased upon reception.
Each interpretation is dependent upon perception.
So what is his-story? Who's story? and who is . . . . his?
Does whoever that is really have authority over what we do with our mental images?
Seems as if it's up to us what we feed and believe and what we desire to receive!
With all of this noise based on personal sway.
That may have distorted away from what may have really happened that day.
So now the power of actual history is actually whatever you want your story to consist.
Whatever you choose to put on your own list!
Really? ..Yes! So proceed at your own risk.
Let YOURstory be your own history.

CONCLUSION . . . .
CONFUSION!!

CONCLUSION . . . . THEY CLAIM ONE THING BUT REALLY MEAN ANOTHER!
Each day we hear them talking about peace and "love"
They express looking inside and looking above
But if you look a little bit closer has anything close to the truth been told
Do we really look at the inside as the real beauty we hold?
Most would claim yes but if that is true then explain all the videos
The billion dollar industry of the reality shows
Even a baby is labeled precious because of the way that it looks
And as long as we think it looks good we believe in crooks

CONCLUSION . . . . THEY CLAIM ONE THING BUT REALLY MEAN ANOTHER!
There are selfish people who claim to be so-called lovers
But usually that is only spoken when it involves the covers
Guys look good to females when they have money and a ring.
Females look good to guys when she has a certain face, body, and she is willing.
If she wears an outfit and its revealing and a guy is desperate he calls her sexy
If he chases her down spends his money all around then to a desperate female he becomes sexy.
But if she doesn't easily spread to him she becomes ugly instead
Now he wants to take back his bread . . . . .
And if he isn't willing to spend even more money and become her hubby he becomes really ugly.
All of a sudden she doesn't want him in her bed.
But they both still claim they 'love' each other.
They claim they wouldn't know what to do without each other.
Until it's over . . . . But is it really over?
They both want the other to come over!
Why? Because the urge of that lust is increasing.
Confused state of emotions is mixing.
After a round or two more arguments continue, they call this 'love'?
What most people call 'love' is really selfish attachment and control
Nothing more than lustful desires of the hormonal.

CONCLUSION . . . . THEY CLAIM ONE THING BUT REALLY MEAN ANOTHER THING!

People are confused about the hustle or take a wage from a job

Now to add the government cuts education now people choose to rob

On one side the government claims that people are free

But this same government encourages poverty and negativity

How are people free with this hidden status quo?

With this Babylon patrol attempting to control where we go!

That patrol is not just the cops with the handcuffs

It's the lawyers, bankers, and politicians living it up so lush.

Its confusing that the same people running commercials to vote in this land

Are same ones who support the snakes that are choking the air and choking the man

The snakes that abuse the woman and brainwash the babies

These snakes have the nerve to even say 'love' but the their message is closer to devastating

You can agree or disagree just look out your front door

Ask yourself is your suffering less or is your pain more?

This system claims that we have an equal chance

But that is only as long as your follow their program and dance

CONCLUSION . . . . CONFUSION!!!

+RELEASE+

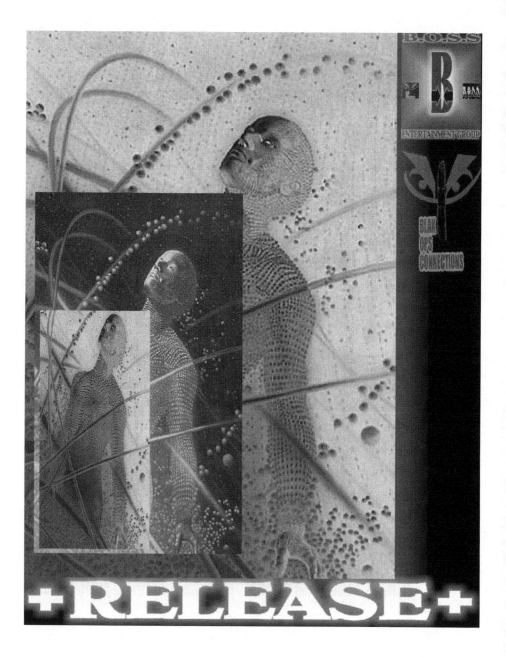

SIMPLE

A reason to be presentable appears
Reasons for stress easily disappears
Its night only visually but its really light and uplifting
Vibe quickly kicking the mind is skipping and drifting
Arrives at the venue eyes scope to see what is on the menu
Solo on the unofficial guest list sounds invited to continue
So what is this? Nothing more than hypersonic bliss!!!
Ears are embracing memories and quality not found to often on mainstream lists!
Besides the sounds, the sights are simple but intricate in delivery.
Easily convinced that this could be a consistent place to deflect misery.
Intrinsically been desiring an experience at the bottom line
Glad to see that there is collection of participation that does not imitate the rotten mind!
The vinyl and digital keeps spinning and not a moment is missed
Even providing eye candy whose physical beauty has been platinum kissed
And to think admission was accessible even status achieved
Didn't think that places like this barely were allowed to be believed
Of course it could have been more flashy more of the chocolate cheese machine
Sponsored by bobbling poultry and hex graphical influences and the asbestos scene
But instead their is hope on a simple release
Hopefully this is not temporary pattern of leads!

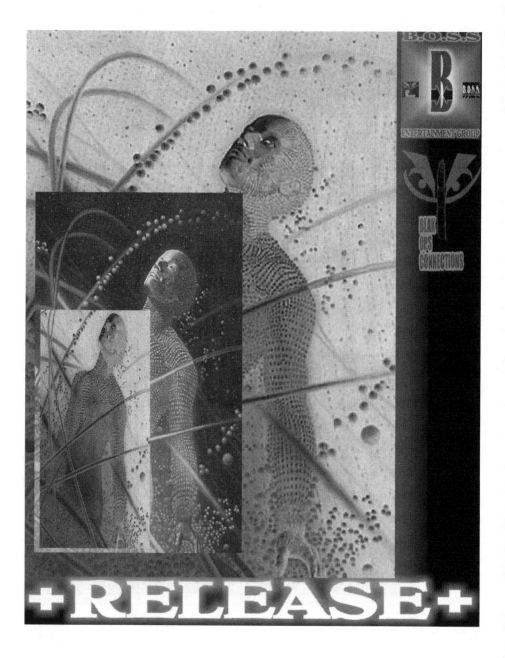

HOPE

It's not all bad!
It will be okay!
Through the rain there are occasional sun-rays.
It's in each success story that is quietly reported.
It's built on each positive progressive movement that is mutually supported.
Hope is the physically healthy baby that begins its journey.
Hope is this same baby that receives assistance in satisfying its yearning.
From the first steps that is taken to the walk of adolescence.
To the sprint of adulthood to the exhale of mature essence.
Hope's first name is the HIGHER that is also called GOD
This is where all hope begins the reason why hands applaud.
That rising smile on faces that excitement anticipating the trophy after running races.
That positive laughter, the sounds of elevation, and the happy feet with quick paces.
All are hope and hope is eternal
Hope has roots deep in the internal
Yes hope has a motor started up by choice
Perspective and responsibility are the hydraulics that raise the hoist
Now look up! Hope is all above us.
It's on the wings of the birds and in the air that we touch.
Look straight ahead! Hope is in front of you!
Walking forward to a positive goal leaving negative control in the distant view.
Now that you walked forward look behind you very carefully.
There is a universe of faith encouraging you consistently.
Look down! Yes hope is even down there.
Hope is the reason why we can walk on strong ground with that confident air!
With all this hope around there is no reason to despair.
Even with many problems all around . . . . HOPE IS EVERYWHERE!

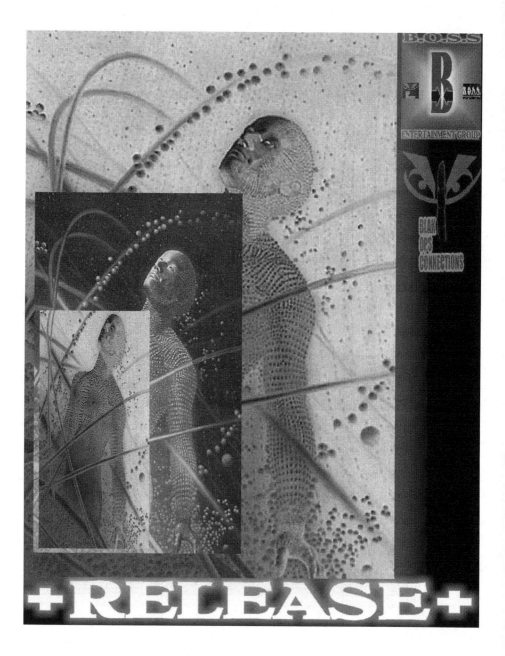

FREEDOMMMMMMMM!!

No strains no clutter no chains space now remains
no interference in the frame success and progress may now accelerate and be
maintained
See the vision extra clear borders have disappeared
low in the drama low in the stress and definitely very low in the fear
As stated before the path of the strong remains narrow to walk
There was too many walking the wide path writing lowercase letters with weak
chalk communicating the words of the lost
Distracted was the focus and the obstacles were placed by the hopeless
Screaming for attention and begging to be noticed
It was and is too much one man with a million claws pulling in different
directions
usually ending up with the common goal of attempting to satisfy selfish affections
Elevation was a mission and this mission involved boot camp
Training was extra hard thank GOD for an opportunity to escape this spot on
the map
Bags and boxes are packed up a brand new address reads
The sunlight is blinding in the spacious outside walking on the grass and the
weeds
Waving hello to a passerby reflecting on brand new origins
Yes this is freedommmmmmm! Now the next phase begins!

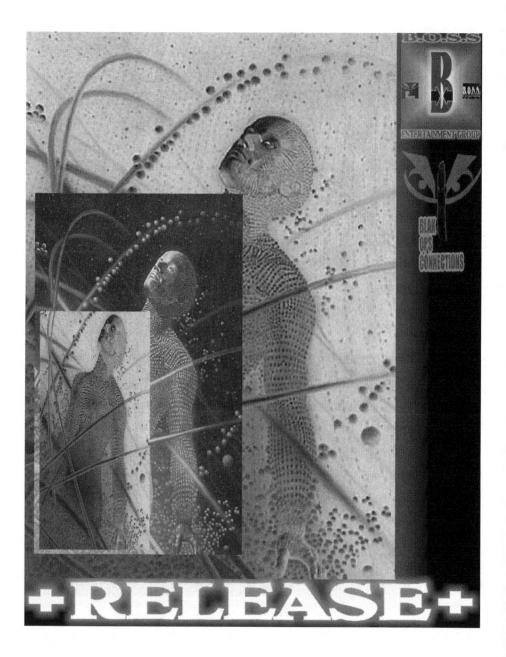

+ALPHA AND OMEGA+

APPRECIATION

No its not deserved but still grace is given
We perpetually stumble but still are perpetually forgiven
Just looking at your real sacrifice is a humbling fact
Trying to pay the unrepayable and not letting off any internal slack
Its not just what you have given or what we have received
Its just the simple presence and what we should believe
But that is their choice to take for granted what is delivered
The protection from the dark and the insulation from the shivers
We lie, cheat, steal, and stay sensitive to the petty
We are flaky, selfish, lustful, greedy, and our foundation is unsteady
Despite all of that you remain in support
Giving us edification in this line that is so short
We have access to so-called legends, icons, celebrities, and stars
But we ignore the lessons and rather focus on flash-in-the-pans, clothes, gossip, and cars
The truth is we are given so much that we don't recognize
We have access to many positive tools and positive vessels that we rather minimize
We are in the presence of fathers, mothers, real-family, real-friends, and historical figures.
We are in the presence of educational resources, financial opportunities, and community centers.
That helped us with our first steps, our first words, and our first definition of this existence.
That was used to give us guidance, trials, punishment, and rewards to help us clear our vision.
Above all else we are embrace by the blanket of the HIGHER!
The pure source of all that is positive something that we should actually admire!
For these reasons and many more when we look at our situations.
Let start by giving appreciation.

THE ONLY ONE TRUE!

All it takes is a whisper of that name
That instantly ignites that combustible flame
Immediately voluntarily paralyzed in the gaze on sight
Surrounded by solar and lunar enclosed by alpha and omega day and night
Songs cant contain words cant express
The complete and utter surrender filled with enough to build a submission fortress
But understand, this is beyond the imagination
This is beyond the physical or mental this is spiritual satisfaction
See this only one true really doesn't require an introduction
Just one word is enough to fill a discussion
We are together we were actually NEVER apart
Redefining and intertwining soul, mind, and heart
Things we should do to show the only one true just due
We should bust through man's impossibilities but even that wouldn't do
There really is not enough not word can deliver
What is so felt so deep with this we should look forward to being a giver
But even what is given is not even missed
And its beyond what we take and way beyond any visual gifts
The only one true deserves and receives from us entire devotion
Full commitment motion unlimited notions without any conditional potions
People try to contain and fight to the death for a facsimile
But there is nothing that compares to the only one true's presence that goes on infinitely
This is truly only the beginning and when this existence is through
Forever united with the only one true!

BOTTOM LINE!

QUICK THOUGHTS!
SLOW THOUGHTS . . . .
POSSESSIVE THOUGHTS?
FAILED RESULTS . . . .
PRESSURE SITUATIONS
SOCIETY FREEBASING!
DANGER FACING . . . .
HEART RACING. . . . .
MIND RACING. . . . .
SPIRITUAL RELAX!!!!!!!!!!!!!!!!!!!
MENTAL FACTS?!?!?!?!?!?!?!?!?
RELATIVE STATEMENTS
UNLIMITED REPLACEMENTS!!!!!!!!!!
CYCLE REPEATS
VICTORY DEFEATS!!!!!!!!!!!!!!!!!!!!!!!!!!!!!
DEFEATS VICTORIOUS . . . .
RESULTS GLORIOUS!!!!!!!!!!!!!!!!!!!!!!!
BAR RAISED
GOD PRAISED!!!
MAN AMAZED . . . !
PAGE BLAZED
PAGE TURNED
LESSON LEARNED!
MONEY ILLUSION . . . .
SUCCESS EARNED!!!

+END SCENE! . . . . WITH MUCH MORE TO COME!!+

+BONUS SECTION AND BIOS+

B.O.S.S ENTERTAINMENT GROUP

These are the basics of B.O.S.S Entertainment Group.

1.B.O.S.S Entertainment Group is a production, general entertainment and general media group that is a division of Blak.Ops.Connections that has existed since 1999.

2.Blak.Ops.Connections is a diverse service, product, supply, and information company established in Detroit, Michigan and provides its diverse business services primarily in the midwest and south United States regions. Feel free to visit www.soundclick.com/blakops, members.soundclick.com/blakops, youtube-blakops24, or just goggle-Blak.Ops.Connections for even more information.

3.B.O.S.S Entertainment Group is a production brand that presents various live performance, social, promotional, and sound events throughout the Metro Detroit Area, the Great Lakes Area, and beyond.

4.B.O.S.S Entertainment Group has a core production group that primarily presents the best of the local Detroit Artists including King Mellowman and Mellow Runnings, King Kuhz, the B.O.S.S Experience, and many other private and public events with artists of diverse genres.

5.Currently B.O.S.S Entertainment Group is expanding operations further in many areas to benefit the arts' community, inner city communities, positive youth movements, and beyond. We are establishing opportunities for those of extreme talent and cooperation to become involved with us!

6.For further information about your interested involvement or general inquiries, feel free to visit http://www.soundclick.com/bands/default.cfm?bandID=398810 or google-Blak.Ops.Connections and search B.O.S.S. Entertainment Group.

BLAK.OPS.CONNECTIONS

These are the basics of Blak.Ops.Connections.

1.Blak.Ops.Connections is an entertainment, production, information, and general media company that has existed since 1999.

2.Blak.Ops.Connections is established in Detroit, Michigan and provides its diverse business services primarily in the midwest and south United States regions. Feel free to visit www.soundclick.com/blakops, members.soundclick.com/blakops, youtube-blakops24, or just goggle-Blak.Ops.Connections for even more information.

3.Blak.Ops.Connections has a core production membership of three talented music producers that cover its mission of providing diverse musical genres. These members include: Cofidential Ice-Hip-Hop, Caribbean, and Pop, Ominous-Dance, Electronica, Pop, Techno, and Hip-Hop, and Oblique-Jazz, R&B, Neo-Soul, Funk, Soul, and Blues.

4.Since 1999, Blak.Ops.Connections has featured many products such as events, CDs, videos, shows and performers. These products have individually peformed and has been featured in many productions around the entire world including appearances in Carnegie Hall, Cobo Hall, The Palace of Auburn Hills, Hollywood Bowl, and various European and foreign venues.

5.Currently Blak.Ops.Connections is seeking to expand operations further in many areas to benefit the arts' community, inner city communities, positive youth movements, and beyond. We are establishing opportunities for those of extreme talent and cooperation to become involved with us!

6.For further information about your interested involvement, contact your Blak.Ops.Connections representative that has met with you or a network affiliate representative at network events. Further contact information will be given.

+N.EVA.MOLDEN+

+AUTHOR BIO+

N. Eva Molden is a motivator and a beautiful human being from Jacksonville, Florida. Since high school, Molden has been involved in improving community and education environments ranging from Arlington, Georgia to Detroit, Michigan to Bloomington, Indiana, to Kansas City, Missouri to Jacksonville, Florida. Molden is also a college educated, world educated, social motivated, and a HIGHER (GOD) motivated individual. Most importantly, Molden is a spiritual-centered and a GOD-centered person who genuinely believes in group over self and improvement over settling.

+RESPONSIBILITY+